UNDERSTANDING THE COFFEE COOKBOOK

A Comprehensive Guide To Mouth-Watering,

Easy Coffee Recipes To Prepare At Home For

Healthy Eating

Luigi Russo

Let's start!

Table of Contents

Health Benefits of Coffee

285 Delicious Recipes

Health Benefits of Coffee

Let's face it. Most of us are bleary eyed, stumbling about with feet dragging when we first wake up in the morning. Yet, when that delightfully rich, and oh so tantalizing coffee aroma tickles our nostrils we schlep, yawning and stretching in its direction. Not only is the smell of coffee a great eye opener, recent studies show that consuming up to three 8-ounce cups of coffee a day has proven health benefits. Let's take a look at a few.

1. Helps fight disease. Caffeine may help protect our brain cells from damage that causes Parkinson's, dementia, and Alzheimer's. Also the antioxidants in coffee could, actually, help prevent liver disease.

2. Gives the brain a boost. Coffee keeps you alert when you may otherwise feel drowsy. Try drinking a cup before an exam or if you have a long drive to sharpen your memory and to stay alert.

3. Helps you lose weight. Caffeine consumption can speed up metabolism and the fat-burning process, which also helps lower the risk of obesity. It is also one of the lowest calorie drinks you can choose.

4. Lowers risk of diabetes. Drinking just one cup of coffee a day - caffeinated or decaf - can decrease the risk of developing diabetes by 13%. But at 12 cups a day, the risk of getting diabetes is slashed by 67%. While these are staggering results, you should consult your doctor before taking the 12-cup a day challenge and always consume caffeine in moderation.

5. Coffee may help with depression. People who consume four or more cups of coffee a day are 10% less likely to be depressed than someone who doesn't drink coffee at all, says a joint study from the National Institutes of Health and the AARP. Strangely the same benefits are not

found in other caffeinated beverages, such as colas whose consumers are linked to a higher risk for depression. Since studies show that black coffee has the highest benefits, perhaps it is the high sugar content in cola that places its consumers at such a high risk for depression.

6. It might be good for your liver. Studies suggest that caffeine helps the liver regulate itself. A person's risk of developing Primary sclerosing cholangitis (PSC), (a rare autoimmune disease that can lead to cirrhosis of the liver, liver failure, and even cancer.), with regular coffee consumption is reduced, says research this month by the Mayo Clinic. Also, a separate 22-year study of 125K people discovered that those who drank at least one cup of coffee a day were 20% less likely to develop alcoholic cirrhosis.

With its brain and metabolism boosting power as well as its disease and disorder fighting properties coffee may be just the super-juice you need with your daily morning meal. When you say you need your morning, you now have a whole new (and beneficial) set of reasons to place behind that statement.

Remember if you suffer from high blood pressure, anxiety, or have an over active thyroid you may want to check with your doctor before drinking coffee. In addition, if you have trouble sleeping it's best to avoid caffeine consumption at least 4 hours before bedtime.

71 Delicious Recipes

Maple Nut Coffee Cake

Ingredients

- 1 (16 ounce) package hot roll mix
- 3 tablespoons sugar
- 3/4 cup warm water (120 to 130 degrees F)
- 1 egg
- 1 teaspoon maple flavoring 1/2 cup butter or margarine, melted, divided
  FILLING:
- 1/2 cup sugar
- 1 teaspoon ground cinnamon 1/2 teaspoon maple flavoring 1/3 cup chopped walnuts
  GLAZE:
- 1 1/2 cups confectioners' sugar
- 1/4 teaspoon maple flavored extract
- 1 tablespoon milk

Directions

In a large bowl, combine flour packet and yeast from hot roll mix. Add sugar. Stir in water, egg, flavoring and 6 tablespoons butter; mix well. Turn onto a floured surface; knead until smooth and elastic, 2-3 minutes. Place in a greased bowl; turn once to grease top.

Cover and let rise in a warm place until doubled, 45-60 minutes. For filling, combine sugar, cinnamon and flavoring. Add nuts; set aside. Divide dough into thirds.

On a lightly floured surface, roll out one portion to a 12-in. circle; place on a greased 12-in. pizza pan. Brush with some of the remaining butter.

Sprinkle with a third of the filling. Repeat, forming two more layers, ending with filling. Pinch dough around outer edge to seal. Mark a 2-in. circle in center of dough (do nut cut through).

Cut from outside edge just to the 2-in. circle, forming 16 wedges. Twist each wedge five to six times. Cover and let rise until doubled, 30-45 minutes.
Bake at 375 degrees F for 20-25 minutes or until golden brown. Cool on wire rack. Combine glaze ingredients; drizzle over warm coffee cake.

Cinnamon Coffee Cake

Ingredients

- 1 cup brown sugar
- 1 cup white sugar
- 2 1/4 cups all-purpose flour 3/4 cup butter, melted
- 1 teaspoon vanilla extract
- 1 teaspoon baking soda
- 1 teaspoon baking powder
- 2 teaspoons ground cinnamon
- 1/2 teaspoon ground ginger
- 1 egg
- 1 cup buttermilk
- 1/4 cup confectioners' sugar

Directions

Preheat oven to 375 degrees F (190 degrees C). Lightly grease and flour a 9x5 inch baking pan.

In a large bowl, combine brown sugar, white sugar and flour. Stir in melted butter until mixture resembles coarse crumbs. Add vanilla extract. Mix in baking soda, baking powder, cinnamon and ginger. Reserve 1/4 cup this mixture to be used as topping.

In a separate bowl, beat together egg and buttermilk; stir slowly into flour mixture. Pour batter into prepared pan. Sprinkle batter with reserved topping.

Bake in preheated oven for 20 to 30 minutes, until a toothpick inserted into center of the cake comes out clean. Sprinkle with powdered sugar and serve.

Blueberry Coffee Cake I

Ingredients

- 1 cup packed brown sugar 2/3 cup all-purpose flour
- 1 teaspoon ground cinnamon 1/2 cup butter
- 2 cups all-purpose flour
- 2 teaspoons baking powder 1/2 teaspoon salt
- 1/2 cup butter
- 1 cup white sugar 1 egg
- 1 teaspoon vanilla extract 1/2 cup milk
- 1 cup fresh blueberries
- 1/4 cup confectioners' sugar for dusting

Directions

Heat oven to 350 degrees F (175 degrees C). Coat a Bundt pan well with cooking spray. Make the streusel topping: Mix 1 brown cup sugar, 2/3 cup flour, and cinnamon in a medium bowl. Cut in 1/2 cup butter or margarine; topping mixture will be crumbly. Set aside.

For the cake: Beat 1/2 cup butter or margarine in large bowl until creamy; add 1 cup white sugar, and beat until fluffy. Beat in egg and vanilla. Whisk together 2 cups flour, baking powder, and salt; add alternately with the milk to the creamed mixture, beating well after each addition.

Spread half the batter in the prepared pan. Cover with berries, and add remaining batter by tablespoons.

Cover with streusel topping. Bake at 350 degrees F (175 degrees C) for 55 to 60 minutes, until deep golden brown. Remove pan to wire rack to cool. Invert onto a plate after cake has cooled, and dust with confectioners' sugar.

Rhubarb Coffee Cake

Ingredients

- 1/2 cup shortening
- 1 1/2 cups packed brown sugar 1 egg
- 2 cups all-purpose flour
- 1 teaspoon baking soda 1/2 teaspoon salt
- 1 cup sour cream
- 2 cups diced fresh or frozen rhubarb, thawed
- TOPPING:
- 1/2 cup packed brown sugar 1/2 cup chopped walnuts
- 1 tablespoon butter or margarine, melted
- 1 teaspoon ground cinnamon

Directions

In a mixing bowl, cream shortening and brown sugar. Beat in the egg. Combine flour, baking soda and salt; add to the creamed mixture alternately with sour cream. Fold in rhubarb. Pour into two greased 8-in. square baking dishes.

Combine the topping ingredients; sprinkle over batter. Bake at 350 degrees F for 40-45 minutes or until toothpick inserted near the center comes out clean.

Cool on wire racks. May be frozen for up to 6 months.

Coffee Smoother

Ingredients

- 1/2 cup coffee 1/4 cup milk
- 1/2 cup chocolate ice cream
- 1 tablespoon cinnamon 1/4 cup ice cubes

Directions

Place the coffee, milk, ice cream, cinnamon, and ice cubes in the bowl of a blender; puree until smooth.

Ben Lippen School Coffee Cake (Mrs. Hathaway's

Ingredients

- 1/4 cup butter
- 1/3 cup white sugar 1 egg
- 1/2 teaspoon vanilla extract
- 1 1/2 cups all-purpose flour 1/4 teaspoon salt
- 2 teaspoons baking powder 2/3 cup milk
- 2 tablespoons all-purpose flour
- 2 tablespoons butter
- 5 tablespoons white sugar
  1/2 teaspoon ground cinnamon

Directions

Preheat the oven to 375 degrees F (190 degrees C).In a large bowl, cream together 1/4 cup butter and 1/3 cup of sugar until smooth. Beat in egg and vanilla until well blended.

Combine 1 1/2 cups of flour, salt and baking powder; stir into the creamed mixture alternately with the milk. Spread evenly in a 9x9 inch baking pan.In a small bowl, stir together 2 tablespoons flour, 5 tablespoons sugar, and cinnamon.

Add 2 tablespoons of butter, and pinch into the dry mixture using your fingers until the mixture is crumbly.
Sprinkle over the top of the cake. Bake for 25 minutes in the preheated oven, until a knife inserted into the center comes out clean.

Traditional Coffee Cake

Ingredients

- 1 (.25 ounce) package active dry yeast
- 1/2 cup warm water
- 1 cup scalded milk
- 3 eggs
- 1/2 cup white sugar 1/2 teaspoon salt
- 4 cups all-purpose flour
- 1/2 cup butter, melted
- 1 cup white sugar
- 3 tablespoons ground cinnamon 1/2 cup butter, melted

Directions

Preheat oven to 400 degrees F (200 degrees C). Dissolve yeast in 1/2 cup lukewarm water. In a large bowl, mix milk, eggs, 1/2 cup sugar and salt. Mix in 1/2 cup melted butter.

Add dissolved yeast mixture. Add the flour and mix well. Turn dough out on floured board. Knead until smooth, about 10 to 15 minutes. Place in greased bowl, and cover.

Let rise in warm place until double in volume, about 1 1/2 to 2 hours. Punch dough down. Turn over, and let rise again for 45 minutes. In a small bowl, combine 1 cup sugar and 3 tablespoons ground cinnamon. Form dough into walnut-sized balls. Dip each ball in melted butter, and roll in cinnamon sugar. Pile loosely into a 10 inch Bundt pan.

Cover and let rise again until about double in volume. Bake for 10 minutes at 400 degrees F (200 degrees C). Reduce temperature to 350 degrees F (175 degrees C), and continue baking an additional 30 minutes, or until golden brown.

Sour Cream Banana Coffee Cake

Ingredients

- 1/4 cup butter or margarine, softened
- 8 tablespoons sugar, divided 1 egg
- 1/4 teaspoon vanilla extract 1/2 cup mashed ripe banana 1/4 cup sour cream
- 1 cup all-purpose flour
- 1/2 teaspoon baking powder 1/2 teaspoon baking soda 1/8 teaspoon salt
- 1/4 cup chopped walnuts
- 1/4 teaspoon ground cinnamon

Directions

In a small mixing bowl, cream butter and 6 tablespoons sugar. Beat in egg and vanilla. Stir in banana and sour cream. Combine the flour, baking powder, baking soda and salt; gradually add to creamed mixture. Combine the walnuts, cinnamon and remaining sugar.

Spoon half of batter into a greased 6-cup fluted tube pan. Sprinkle with nut mixture; top with remaining batter. Bake at 350 degrees F for 32-38 minutes or until a toothpick inserted near the center comes out clean.

Cool for 10 minutes before removing from pan to a wire rack.

Pecan Coffee Cake

Ingredients

- 1 (18.25 ounce) package yellow cake mix
- 1 (3.4 ounce) package instant vanilla pudding mix
- 4 eggs
- 1 cup sour cream
- 1/3 cup vegetable oil
- 2 teaspoons vanilla extract 2/3 cup chopped pecans 1/3 cup sugar
- 2 teaspoons ground cinnamon 1/2 cup confectioners' sugar
- 2 tablespoons orange juice

Directions

In a mixing bowl, combine the first six ingredients. Beat on medium speed for 2 minutes. Pour into a greased 13-in. x 9-in. x 2-in. baking pan. Combine pecans, sugar and cinnamon; sprinkle over batter.
Cut through with a knife to swirl.

Bake at 350 degrees F for 30-35 minutes or until a toothpick inserted near the center comes out clean. In a small bowl, combine confectioners' sugar and orange juice until smooth; drizzle over warm coffee cake.

Coffee Mallow Dessert

Ingredients

- 8 cream-filled chocolate cookies, crushed
- 2 tablespoons butter or margarine, melted
- 1/2 cup hot brewed coffee
- 16 marshmallows
- 1/2 cup whipping cream
- 1 tablespoon confectioners' sugar 1/2 teaspoon vanilla extract

Directions

Combine cookie crumbs and butter; set aside 1 tablespoon for topping. Press remaining crumb mixture onto the bottom and up the sides of two lightly greased 10-oz. custard cups; set aside.

Place coffee and eight marshmallows in a blender; cover and process until smooth. Add the remaining marshmallows; cover and refrigerate in the blender for 2 hours or until cold. Process again until smooth; transfer to a bowl.

In a mixing bowl, beat whipping cream until soft peaks form. Gradually add sugar and vanilla, beating until stiff peaks form. Gently fold into coffee mixture. Spoon into prepared cups; sprinkle with reserved crumbs. Refrigerate for at least 1-2 hours before serving.

Coffee Butter Frosting

Ingredients

- 1 1/2 cups confectioners' sugar
- 1 tablespoon unsweetened cocoa powder
- 1/3 cup butter or margarine, softened
- 1 tablespoon strong brewed coffee

Directions

In a small bowl, stir together the confectioners sugar and cocoa powder. In another bowl, beat the butter until creamy, gradually beat in the sugar mixture, being sure to scrape the bottom of the bowl, occasionally.

Finally stir in the coffee, and beat until smooth.

Sour Cream Coffee Cake II

Ingredients

- 1 cup white sugar
- 1 cup butter, softened
- 3 eggs
- 2 cups all-purpose flour
- 1 1/2 teaspoons baking powder
- 1 1/2 teaspoons baking soda 1/2 cup sour cream
- 1 cup chopped walnuts 3/4 cup white sugar
- 2 teaspoons ground cinnamon

Directions

Preheat oven to 350 degrees F (175 degrees C). Lightly grease one 8x12 inch pan.In a large bowl, cream together 1 cup of the white sugar with 1 cup butter.

Add the eggs and beat well. Mix in the flour, baking soda, baking powder, and sour cream, stir until just combined. Pour 1/2 of the batter into the prepared pan then sprinkle with 3/4 of the filling.

Pour the remaining cake batter on top and sprinkle top with the remaining filling. Bake at 350 degrees F (175 degrees C) for 40 minutes.
To Make Filling:
Combine chopped nuts, ground cinnamon, and 3/4 cup white sugar and mix well.

Streusel Coffee Cake

Ingredients

- 1/2 cup butter or margarine 3/4 cup sugar
- 1 teaspoon vanilla extract
- 3 eggs
- 2 cups all-purpose flour
- 1 teaspoon baking powder
- 1 teaspoon baking soda
- 1 cup sour cream
  STREUSEL TOPPING:
- 1 cup chopped pecans
- 1 cup packed brown sugar
- 1/2 teaspoon ground cinnamon
- 6 tablespoons butter or margarine, softened
  ICING:
- 1 cup sifted confectioners' sugar
- 1 tablespoon butter or margarine, softened
- 1/2 teaspoon vanilla extract
- 3 tablespoons milk

Directions

In a mixing bowl, cream butter for 30 seconds. Add sugar and vanilla; beat until well combined. Add eggs, one at a time, beating well after each addition.

Combine flour, baking powder and soda; add to creamed mixture alternately with sour cream. Spoon half of batter into a greased 10-in. tube pan. Combine topping ingredients; sprinkle half over batter.

Add remaining batter and topping. Bake at 350 degrees F for 45 minutes or until done.

Cool in pan on wire rack for 10 minutes before removing from pan to cool completely. For icing, combine all ingredients; drizzle over cake.

Moravian Sugar Coffee Cake

Ingredients

- 1 pound potatoes, peeled and chopped
- 2 cups water
- 1/2 teaspoon salt
- 1/2 cup white sugar
- 1/2 teaspoon ground mace 1/2 cup butter
- 1 egg
- 3 1/4 cups all-purpose flour
- 2 tablespoons active dry yeast
- 3/4 pound dark brown sugar
- 4 tablespoons ground cinnamon 3/4 cup butter, diced
- 1 teaspoon evaporated milk

Directions

Place potatoes and water in a medium saucepan. Bring to a boil. Boil until the potatoes are tender. Drain, reserving 1/2 cup water, and mash. Place mashed potatoes, reserved water, salt, sugar, mace, butter, egg, flour and yeast in the pan of a bread machine in the order recommended by the manufacturer. Select dough cycle; press Start. Spread dough on an 11x13 inch baking sheet.

Cover with a damp cloth and let rise in a warm place until doubled in volume, about 1 hour.
Preheat oven to 350 degrees F (175 degrees C).
Poke several medium holes in the dough and fill with brown sugar and butter. Sprinkle the dough with cinnamon and evaporated milk.

Bake in the preheated oven 20 to 25 minutes.

Apple Nut Coffee Cake

Ingredients

- 1 cup sugar
- 1/2 cup unsweetened applesauce 1/4 cup egg substitute
- 1 cup all-purpose flour
- 1 teaspoon ground cinnamon 1/2 teaspoon baking powder ½ teaspoon baking soda
- 1/4 teaspoon salt
- 1 cup sliced, peeled tart apples 1/2 cup coarsely chopped pecans TOPPING:
- 1/4 cup packed brown sugar 1/4 cup chopped pecans
- 1 tablespoon butter or stick margarine, melted
- 1/4 teaspoon ground cinnamon

Directions

In a mixing bowl, combine the sugar, applesauce and egg substitute; mix well. Combine the flour, cinnamon, baking powder, baking soda and salt; add to the applesauce mixture. Stir in apple and pecans. Spread in an 8-in. square baking dish coated with nonstick cooking spray. In a bowl, combine the brown sugar, pecans, butter and cinnamon; sprinkle over apple mixture.

Bake at 350 degrees F for 30-35 minutes or until a toothpick inserted near the center comes out clean. Cool on a wire rack.

Almond Orange Streusel Coffee Cake

Ingredients

- Streusel:
- 1 cup packed brown sugar
- 1 cup sliced almonds
- 1/4 cup all-purpose flour
- 3 tablespoons butter, melted
- 1 teaspoon freshly grated orange zest
- Cake:
- 1/2 cup butter, softened 1/2 cup white sugar
- 3 eggs
- 1 teaspoon freshly grated orange zest
- 1/2 teaspoon vanilla extract
- 2 cups all-purpose flour
- 1 teaspoon baking powder
- 1 teaspoon baking soda 2/3 cup orange juice
- Glaze:
- 5 teaspoons orange juice
- 1 cup confectioners' sugar

Directions

Preheat oven to 350 degrees F (175 degrees C). Grease a 9 inch tube pan. In a medium bowl, mix brown sugar, almonds, and flour. Stir in butter and 1 teaspoon orange zest, and set aside. In a separate medium bowl, thoroughly beat together butter and sugar with an electric mixer.

Mix in eggs one at a time. Beat in remaining teaspoon orange zest and vanilla extract. In a large bowl, mix flour, baking powder, and baking soda. With an electric mixer set to Low, alternately mix in egg mixture and 2/3 cups orange juice to make a batter. Spoon 1/2 the batter into the prepared 9 inch tube pan.

Top with 1/2 the brown sugar mixture.

Cover with remaining batter, and top with remaining brown sugar mixture. Bake 25 to 35 minutes in the preheated oven, until a toothpick inserted in the center comes out clean. Turn out onto a wire rack to cool.

Mix 5 teaspoons orange juice and confectioner's sugar in a small bowl, and use to glaze the cooled cake.

Famous No Coffee Pumpkin Latte

Ingredients

- 1 cup pumpkin puree
- 1 quart milk
- 1/4 cup white sugar
- 1 teaspoon ground cinnamon
- 1 tablespoon vanilla extract

Directions

Combine pumpkin, milk, sugar, cinnamon, and vanilla in a large saucepan over medium heat.

Use a whisk to blend well. Heat to a simmer; do not boil.

Cinnamon Swirl Bundt Coffee Cake

Ingredients

- 1 cup sour cream 3/4 cup butter
- 1 1/2 cups white sugar
- 2 1/2 cups all-purpose flour 1/2 cup chopped walnuts
- 1 teaspoon baking soda
- 1 teaspoon baking powder
- 1 teaspoon vanilla extract
- 3 eggs
- 1 tablespoon ground cinnamon 1/4 cup white sugar

Directions

Preheat oven to 400 degrees F (205 degrees C). Lightly grease one 10 inch bundt pan. Cream 1 1/2 cups white sugar together with eggs until well blended. Add sour cream and butter or margarine and beat well.

Add flour, baking soda, and baking powder and mix well. Stir in vanilla and the chopped nuts.Mix the remaining 1/4 cup of white sugar with the cinnamon. Pour half of the batter into the prepared pan. Sprinkle generously with the cinnamon sugar mixture.

Cover with remaining cake batter. Bake at 400 degrees F (205 degrees C) for 8 minutes. Lower heat to 350 degrees F (175 degrees C) and bake for an additional 40 minutes.

Christine's Coffee Liqueur Cookies

Ingredients

- 2 teaspoons instant coffee granules
- 2 tablespoons coffee-flavored liqueur
- 1 cup butter, softened
- 3/4 cup packed brown sugar
- 1 cup white sugar
- 2 eggs
- 2 1/2 cups all-purpose flour 1/3 cup unsweetened cocoa powder
- 1/2 teaspoon baking soda 1/4 teaspoon salt
- 2 cups semisweet chocolate chips

Directions

Preheat oven to 300 degrees F (150 degrees C). In a small bowl, dissolve instant coffee crystals into the coffee liqueur; set aside. In a large bowl, cream together the butter, brown sugar, and white sugar. Gradually add eggs and coffee mixture while mixing.

Sift together the flour, cocoa, baking soda, and salt; stir into the creamed mixture. Finally, stir in the chocolate chips.
Drop dough by rounded tablespoonfuls onto a cookie sheet.

Cookies should be at least 2 inches apart. Bake for 23 to 25 minutes. Immediately transfer cookies to cooling rack after baking. These keep well at room temperature or refrigerated.

Cinnamon-Walnut Coffee Cake

Ingredients

- 1/4 cup shortening
- 1 cup sugar
- 2 eggs
- 1 1/2 teaspoons vanilla extract
- 2 cups all-purpose flour
- 1 1/2 teaspoons baking powder
- 1 teaspoon salt
- 1 cup milk
  TOPPING:
- 1/2 cup all-purpose flour 1/4 cup sugar
- 1 teaspoon ground cinnamon
- 3 tablespoons cold butter
- 1 1/2 cups chopped walnuts

Directions

In a mixing bowl, cream shortening and sugar. Add eggs, one at a time, beating well after each addition. Beat in vanilla. Combine the flour, baking powder and salt; add to the creamed mixture alternately with the milk.

Transfer to a greased 9-in. square baking pan. In a bowl, combine the flour, sugar and cinnamon; cut in butter until mixture resembles coarse crumbs. Stir in nuts. Sprinkle over top.

Bake at 350 degrees F for 55-60 minutes or until a toothpick inserted near the center comes out clean. Cool on a wire rack.

Billy's Favorite Gingerbread Spiced Coffee Syrup

Ingredients

- 1 cup water
- 1 cup sugar
- 1 tablespoon honey
- 1 (1 inch) piece fresh ginger root, sliced
- 1 cinnamon stick, broken into large pieces
- 8 whole cloves
- 1/2 teaspoon whole allspice berries
- 1/2 teaspoon whole peppercorns 1/2 teaspoon ground nutmeg

Directions

In a saucepan over medium-high heat, combine water, sugar, and honey. Stir in ginger, cinnamon stick, cloves, allspice, peppercorns, and nutmeg; bring to a boil.

Reduce heat, cover, and simmer for 25 to 30 minutes. Let cool for 20 minutes, then strain through a fine mesh sieve, or double layer cheesecloth.

Coffee Liqueur Ice Cream Pie

Ingredients

- 1 1/8 cups chocolate wafer cookies, crushed
- 1/2 cup unsalted butter, melted
- 6 tablespoons coffee-flavored liqueur
- 1 teaspoon instant espresso coffee powder
- 3 ounces semisweet chocolate, chopped
- 1 tablespoon unsalted butter
- 1 pint vanilla ice cream, softened
- 2 tablespoons coffee-flavored liqueur
- 1 pint chocolate ice cream, softened
- 2 tablespoons coffee-flavored liqueur
- 3/4 cup whipped cream, beaten stiff

Directions

Preheat oven to 325 degrees F (165 degrees C). In a medium bowl, stir together the cookie crumbs and melted butter. Press mixture evenly onto bottom and sides of a 9 inch pie pan. Bake crust in oven for 10 minutes. Remove from oven and cool completely.

In a small saucepan, heat 6 tablespoons of liqueur and espresso powder over low heat. Heat until warm and powder is dissolved. Stir in chocolate and 1 tablespoon of butter until mixture is melted and smooth. Allow to cool completely.

Place vanilla ice cream into mixing bowl with 2 tablespoons of coffee liqueur. Using an electric mixer, blend together on low speed.

Spread over bottom of cooled crust and freeze until firm. Then spread cooled chocolate mixture over frozen ice cream. Freeze pie until firm.

Blend together chocolate ice cream and 2 tablespoons liqueur.

Spread chocolate ice cream mixture over frozen chocolate sauce in pie. Freeze until firm.

Serve pie with a decorative piped border of whipped cream around the inside edge of the pie.

Coffee Flavored Liqueur III

Ingredients

- 2 cups water
- 1 1/4 cups white sugar
- 2 tablespoons vanilla extract
- 2 tablespoons fresh ground coffee beans
- 2 1/2 cups vodka

Directions

In a saucepan over medium heat, combine water, sugar, vanilla and ground coffee. Bring to a boil, reduce heat to low, and simmer for 10 minutes, stirring occasionally.

Allow to cool, then remove grounds through a strainer. When cool, stir in vodka. Pour into a liquor bottle, and keep in a cool place.

Nutty Lemon Coffee Cake

Ingredients

- 1 cup butter or margarine, softened
- 1 cup sugar
- 3 eggs
- 1 cup sour cream
- 1 teaspoon vanilla extract
- 1 teaspoon lemon extract
- 2 1/2 cups all-purpose flour
- 2 1/2 teaspoons baking powder
- 1 teaspoon baking soda 1/8 teaspoon salt
- TOPPING:
- 1 cup ground pecans 1/2 cup sugar
- 1 teaspoon ground cinnamon

Directions

In a mixing bowl, cream butter and sugar. Add eggs, one at a time, beating well after each addition. In another bowl, mix sour cream and extracts.Combine flour, baking powder, baking soda and salt; add to creamed mixture alternately with sour cream mixture.

Mix well. Spread half in a greased 13-in. x 9-in. x 2-in. baking pan. Combine topping ingredients; sprinkle half over batter. Carefully spread remaining batter on top; sprinkle with remaining topping.

Bake at 350 degrees F for 30-35 minutes or until cake tests done.

Fresh Berry Coffeecake

Ingredients

- 2 cups fresh raspberries
- 6 tablespoons brown sugar
- 2 cups all-purpose flour 2/3 cup white sugar
- 1 teaspoon baking powder 1/2 teaspoon baking soda ¼ teaspoon salt
- 1 cup sour cream
- 1/4 cup butter, melted
- 2 teaspoons vanilla extract
- 2 eggs
- 2 cups toasted, chopped pecans
- 2 teaspoons milk
- 1/2 teaspoon vanilla extract
- 1/2 cup confectioners' sugar

Directions

Preheat oven to 350 degrees F (175 degrees C). Spray a 10 inch Bundt cake pan with non-stick cooking spray. Stir together raspberries and brown sugar; set aside. In a separate bowl, mix together flour sugar, baking powder, baking soda and salt; set aside. In a third bowl, cream together sour cream, butter and 2 teaspoons vanilla.

Beat in eggs one at a time. Stir in flour mixture just until Moist.Sprinkle 1/2 cup of berries and 1 cup pecans in pan, pour in half of the batter. Pour on the remaining berries and remaining cup of pecans.

Spread the remaining batter over the berries. Bake in preheated oven for 35 to 40 minutes, or until a toothpick inserted into center of the cake comes out clean.

While cake bakes, mix the frosting. In a small bowl, stir together 2 teaspoons milk, 1/2 teaspoon vanilla and 1/2 cup confectioners' sugar.

Remove cake from pan and let cool 20 minutes before frosting.

Berry Good Coffee Cake

Ingredients

- 1 cup all-purpose flour 1/3 cup white sugar
- 1/2 teaspoon baking powder 1/4 teaspoon baking soda ¼ teaspoon salt
- 1 egg
- 1/2 cup reduced-fat plain yogurt
- 2 tablespoons butter, melted
- 1 teaspoon vanilla extract
- 3 tablespoons brown sugar
- 1 cup fresh or frozen raspberries
- 1 tablespoon slivered almonds
- Glaze
- 1/4 cup confectioners' sugar
- 1 teaspoon fat free milk
- 1/4 teaspoon vanilla extract

Directions

Preheat oven to 350 degrees F (175 degrees C). Lightly coat an 8 inch round cake pan with nonstick cooking spray.

Sift together the flour, sugar, baking powder, baking soda, and salt in a large bowl. In a separate bowl, whisk together the egg, yogurt, butter, and 1 teaspoon vanilla extract. Stir the egg mixture into the flour until well moistened. Toss the raspberries with the brown sugar in a small bowl.

Pour 2/3 of the batter into the cake pan and sprinkle with the raspberries and almonds. Spoon the remaining batter over the raspberries.

Bake in preheated oven until cake springs back when lightly

touched, 35 to 40 minutes. Set aside to cool.

To make the glaze, stir together the sugar, milk, and 1/4 teaspoon of vanilla extract until smooth. Drizzle glaze over the cooled coffee cake.

Serve at room temperature.

Mocha Cigars with Coffee Cream

Ingredients

CIGARS
- 2 cups sifted confectioners' sugar
- 1 1/4 cups sifted all-purpose flour 1/8 teaspoon salt
- 5/8 cup butter, melted and cooled
- 1 vanilla bean, split and scraped
- 6 egg whites, room temperature
- 1 tablespoon heavy cream
- 1 1/2 ounces bittersweet chocolate, grated

COFFEE CREAM FILLING
- 1/4 cup coffee flavored liqueur
- 1 1/2 teaspoons instant espresso coffee powder
- 2 1/2 cups heavy cream
- 1/4 cup confectioners' sugar
- 1 1/2 ounces bittersweet chocolate, grated

Directions

In a large bowl, mix 2 cups confectioners' sugar, flour and salt. Make a well in the center and set aside. In another bowl, combine melted butter and vanilla scrapings.

Pour vanilla butter, egg whites and 1 tablespoon cream into well of dry ingredients. Mix until smooth. Fold in 1 1/2 ounces grated chocolate. Chill in refrigerator 2 hours or overnight. Preheat oven to 400 degrees F (200 degrees C).

Line a baking sheet with waxed paper. Make a stencil by using a utility knife to cut a 4 1/2 inch (11.5 centimeter) circle in the center of a flexible plastic lid. Place the stencil on the baking sheet and spread 2 teaspoons of batter inside circle; remove stencil.
Make 3 circles on a baking sheet. Bake in preheated oven 2

minutes, rotate pan and bake 2 minutes more, until golden. Working quickly, remove cookie from tray with a spatula and roll around the handle of a wooden spoon.

Place rolled cookies on wire rack to cool completely. If cookies harden before rolling, return to oven for 30 seconds to soften. Repeat to use all remaining batter.

To make coffee cream: Beat together coffee liqueur and espresso powder until powder is dissolved.

Beat in 2 1/2 cups cream and 1/4 cup confectioners' sugar until soft peaks form. Refrigerate 15 minutes. Fill cooled cookies with coffee cream using a pastry bag fitted with a 3/8 inch round tip. Dip each end of filled cookies in grated chocolate.

Serve at once, or store in an airtight container up to 3 days.

Coffee Ice Cream

Ingredients

- 1/4 cup sugar
- 1 tablespoon cornstarch
- 1 tablespoon instant coffee granules
- 2 tablespoons butter or margarine, melted
- 1 cup milk
- 1 teaspoon vanilla extract
- 1 (14 ounce) can sweetened condensed milk
- 2 cups whipping cream

Directions

In a saucepan, stir sugar, cornstarch, coffee and butter until blended. Stir in milk. Bring to a boil over medium heat; cook and stir for 2 minutes or until thickened. Remove from the heat; stir in vanilla.

Cool completely. Stir in condensed milk. In a mixing bowl, beat cream until stiff peaks form; fold into milk mixture. Pour into a 9-in. square pan.
Cover and freeze for 6 hours or until firm.

Caramel Apple Coffee Cake

Ingredients

- 3 eggs
- 2 cups sugar
- 1 1/2 cups vegetable oil
- 2 teaspoons vanilla extract
- 3 cups all-purpose flour
- 1 teaspoon salt
- 1 teaspoon baking soda
- 4 cups chopped, peeled apples
- 1 cup coarsely chopped pecans TOPPING:
- 1/2 cup butter or margarine 1/4 cup milk
- 1 cup packed brown sugar Pinch salt

Directions

In a mixing bowl, beat eggs until foamy; gradually add sugar. Blend in oil and vanilla. Combine flour, salt and baking soda; add to egg mixture. Stir in apples and pecans. Pour into a greased 10-in. tube pan; bake at 350 degrees F for 1 hour and 15 minutes or until the cake tests done. Cool in pan on a wire rack for 10 minutes. Remove cake to a serving platter.

For topping, combine all ingredients in a saucepan; boil 3 minutes, stirring constantly. Slowly pour over warm cake (some topping will run down onto the serving plate.)

Spiced Coconut Coffee

Ingredients

- 2 tablespoons ground coffee beans
- 1/2 teaspoon crushed red pepper
- 2 whole cloves
- 1/2 (3 inch) cinnamon stick
- 2 cups water
- 1/2 cup coconut milk
- 2 tablespoons honey

Directions

Combine the ground coffee, red pepper, cloves, and cinnamon stick in a coffee filter set into a drip coffee brewer. Pour the water into the brewer's water reservoir. Set the coffee brewer on to brew.

While the coffee brews, gently warm the coconut milk in a small saucepan over medium-low heat. Stir in the honey until the honey is dissolved. Pour the brewed coffee into the mixture; stir.
Divide the liquid into two mugs to serve.

BREAKSTONE'S Fruit-Filled Coffee Cake

Ingredients

- 1 package (2-layer size) white cake mix
- 1 teaspoon ground cinnamon
- 1 cup BREAKSTONE'S Reduced Fat Sour Cream
- 3 eggs
- 1/4 cup water
- 1 (21 ounce) can cherry pie filling 1/2 cup PLANTERS Sliced
- Almonds, toasted
- 1 cup powdered sugar
- 1 1/2 tablespoons milk

Directions

Heat oven to 350 degrees F. Beat first 5 ingredients with mixer until well blended. Pour into greased and floured 13x9-inch pan; top with spoonfuls of pie filling.

Bake 35 minutes or until toothpick inserted in center comes out clean; sprinkle with nuts.
Cool 10 minutes. Mix sugar and milk; drizzle over cake. Cool completely.

Coffee Almond Crisps

Ingredients

- 1 cup shortening
- 2 cups packed brown sugar
- 2 eggs
- 1/2 cup brewed coffee, room temperature
- 3 1/2 cups all-purpose flour
- 1 teaspoon baking soda
- 1 teaspoon salt
- 1 1/2 teaspoons ground cinnamon, divided
- 1 cup chopped almonds, toasted
- 3 tablespoons sugar

Directions

In a mixing bowl, cream shortening and brown sugar. Add eggs, one at a time, beating well after each addition. Beat in coffee. Combine flour, baking soda, salt and 1 teaspoon of cinnamon; gradually add to the creamed mixture. Stir in almonds.

Drop by rounded teaspoonfuls 2 in. apart onto ungreased baking sheets. Combine sugar and remaining cinnamon; sprinkle over cookies. Flatten slightly. Bake at 375 degrees F for 10-12 minutes or until firm.
Remove to wire racks to cool.

Upside-Down Coffee Cake

Ingredients

- 1/2 cup butter
- 2 cups light brown sugar
- 3 cups fresh peaches, pitted and sliced
- 2/3 cup margarine
- 1 1/3 cups white sugar
- 4 eggs
- 2 teaspoons vanilla extract
- 1 1/3 cups milk
- 3 1/3 cups all-purpose flour
- 4 teaspoons baking powder 1/2 teaspoon salt
- 1 teaspoon ground cinnamon

Directions

Preheat oven to 350 degrees F (175 degrees C). Use a deep sided 10 inch pan, or wrap the outside of a 10 inch springform pan with aluminum foil to prevent leaking. Sift together the flour, baking powder, salt and cinnamon. Set aside. In a saucepan over medium heat, combine brown sugar and 1/2 cup butter.

Bring to a boil, then pour into bottom of springform pan. Sprinkle with sliced peaches. In a large bowl, cream together 2/3 cup margarine and the white sugar until light and fluffy. Beat in the eggs one at a time, then stir in the vanilla.

Beat in the flour mixture alternately with the milk. Pour batter over caramel and fruit in pan. Bake in the preheated oven for 90 minutes, or until a toothpick inserted into the center of the cake comes out clean.
Cool in pan for 10 minutes, then invert onto serving platter and carefully remove pan. Be extremely careful of hot caramel and fruit juices! Serve warm.

Blueberry Oatmeal Coffee Cake

Ingredients

- 1 1/3 cups all-purpose flour 3/4 cup quick-cooking oats 1/3 cup sugar
- 2 teaspoons baking powder 1/2 teaspoon salt
- 1 egg
- 1/2 cup fat-free milk 1/4 cup canola oil
- 1/4 cup reduced-fat sour cream
- 1 cup fresh or frozen blueberries* STREUSEL TOPPING:
- 1/4 cup quick-cooking oats
- 3 tablespoons all-purpose flour
- 3 tablespoons brown sugar
- 2 tablespoons cold butter or stick margarine

Directions

In a large bowl, combine the flour, oats, sugar, baking powder and salt. In another bowl, beat the egg, milk, oil and sour cream. Stir into dry ingredients just until moistened. Fold in blueberries.

Pour into a 9-in. round baking pan coated with nonstick cooking spray. For topping, in a small bowl, combine the oats, flour and brown sugar; cut in butter until crumbly. Sprinkle over batter.

Bake at 400 degrees F for 20-25 minutes or until a toothpick inserted near the center comes out clean. Cool on a wire rack.

Jewish Coffee Cake

Ingredients

- 1/2 cup butter
- 1 cup white sugar
- 2 eggs
- 2 cups all-purpose flour
- 1 teaspoon baking soda
- 1 teaspoon baking powder
- 1 cup sour cream
- 1 teaspoon vanilla extract
- 1 cup chopped walnuts
- 1/2 cup confectioners' sugar
- 2 teaspoons ground cinnamon
- 2 tablespoons butter, melted

Directions

Preheat oven to 350 degrees F (175 degrees C). Grease and flour a 9x9 inch pan. Combine the flour, baking soda and baking powder; set aside. In a medium bowl, cream together the sugar, butter and eggs until smooth.

Add the flour mixture and beat until smooth. Finally, stir in the sour cream and vanilla. In a separate bowl, combine the nuts, confectioners' sugar and cinnamon.
Spread half of the batter into the 9x9 inch pan. Sprinkle a layer of the nut mixture, then spread the remaining batter and top with the rest of the nut mixture. Spread the melted butter over the top.

Bake for 1 hour in the preheated oven, until cake springs back to the touch.

Coffee Flavored Fruit Dip

Ingredients

- 1 (8 ounce) package cream cheese, softened
- 1 (8 ounce) container sour cream 1/2 cup brown sugar
- 1/3 cup coffee-flavored liqueur
- 1 (8 ounce) container frozen whipped topping, thawed

Directions

Place cream cheese, sour cream, brown sugar and coffee-flavored liqueur in a medium bowl. Blend together with an electric mixer until smooth.

Fold in thawed frozen whipped topping.

Chill in the refrigerator until serving.

Toffee Bar Coffee Cake

Ingredients

- 2 cups all-purpose flour 3/4 cup white sugar
- 3/4 cup brown sugar
- 6 tablespoons butter, softened
- 1 cup milk
- 2 teaspoons baking powder
- 1 teaspoon vanilla extract
- 5 (1.4 ounce) bars chocolate covered toffee bars, chopped
- 1 egg
- 1/2 cup chopped, unsalted dry- roasted peanuts

Directions

Preheat oven to 350 degrees F (175 degrees C). Grease and flour a 9x13 inch pan. Crush toffee bars into small bits and set aside. In a large bowl, combine flour, sugar, brown sugar and butter; mix on low speed with an electric mixer until crumbly. Remove 1/2 cup of crumb mixture and set aside to be used for topping.

Add milk, baking powder, vanilla, egg, and 1/2 cup of the crushed toffee bars; beat at low speed until well-mixed. Increase speed to medium, and beat for 1 minute. Spread batter evenly in 9x13 inch pan. To make the topping: In a small bowl, mix nuts, remaining chopped toffee bars, and reserved 1/2 cup crumb mixture. Sprinkle mixture evenly over batter in pan. Bake for 30 minutes, or until it tests done.

Cool cake completely in pan on rack. Make about 2 1/2 hours before serving, or early the in day.

Apple Cream Coffee Cake

Ingredients

- 1/2 cup chopped walnuts
- 2 teaspoons ground cinnamon
- 1 1/2 cups sugar, divided
- 1/2 cup butter or margarine, softened
- 2 eggs
- 1 teaspoon vanilla extract
- 2 cups all-purpose flour
- 1 teaspoon baking powder 1/2 teaspoon baking soda ½ teaspoon salt
- 1 cup sour cream
- 1 medium apple - peeled, cored and thinly sliced

Directions

Combine nuts, cinnamon and 1/2 cup sugar; set aside. In a large mixing bowl, cream butter; gradually add remaining sugar, beating until light and fluffy. Add eggs, one at a time, beating well after each addition. Blend in vanilla.

Combine dry ingredients; add to creamed mixture alternately with sour cream, beating well after each addition. Spread half of the batter in a well greased 10-in. tube pan with a removable bottom. Top with apple slices; sprinkle with half of the nutmixture. To with remaining batter, then with remaining nut mixture.

Bake at 375 degrees F for 40 minutes or until cake tests done. Remove from oven; let stand 30 minutes. Loosen sides of cake; lift cake with removable bottom from pan. Cool. Before serving, carefully lift cake from pan.

Apricot Danish Coffee Cake

Ingredients

- 1 (18.25 ounce) package white cake mix
- 3 eggs
- 1 1/2 cups sour cream
- 1 (15 ounce) can apricot halves, drained
- 1 tablespoon butter
- 1/2 cup slivered almonds
- 1 (8 ounce) package cream cheese
- 2 tablespoons milk
- 2/3 cup confectioners' sugar
- 2 teaspoons water

Directions

Preheat oven to 350 degrees F (175 degrees C). Grease and flour a 10x15 inch jellyroll pan. Set aside 1/2 cup of the dry cake mix.

In a medium bowl, mix together eggs and sour cream. Stir in the package of cake mix. Batter will be lumpy. Spread batter into the prepared pan.
Using the back of a spoon, make 15 wells in the batter, 3 rows of 5. In another bowl, beat together the cream cheese and milk until fluffy.

Place one tablespoon of the cream cheese mixture into each well. Place 1 apricot half, cut side up, onto each blob of cream cheese.
In a small bowl, combine the 1/2 cup of reserved cake mix with the butter. stir in the butter until the mixture is crumbly. Stir in the slivered almonds, and sprinkle the mixture evenly over the Danish.

Bake for 30 to 35 minutes in the preheated oven, or until a toothpick inserted into the cake comes out clean.

To make the glaze, stir together the confectioners' sugar and water until smooth, adding another teaspoon of water if necessary. Drizzle over the Danish when cool.

Mini Coffee Cakes

Ingredients

- 1/3 cup butter or margarine, softened
- 1/4 cup sugar 1 egg
- 1 1/2 cups all-purpose flour
- 1 (3.4 ounce) package instant vanilla pudding mix
- 1 tablespoon baking powder 1/4 teaspoon salt
- 1 1/4 cups milk
- 1/2 cup chopped walnuts TOPPING:
- 1/2 cup chopped walnuts
- 1/3 cup packed brown sugar
- 2 tablespoons butter or margarine, melted
- 1/4 teaspoon ground cinnamon

Directions

In a mixing bowl, cream the butter and sugar. Beat in egg.
Combine the flour, pudding mix, baking powder and salt; add to the creamed mixture alternately with milk. Beat until blended. Stir in walnuts. Fill paper-lined muffin cups two-thirds full.

Combine topping ingredients; sprinkle over batter.
Bake at 375 degrees for 20-25 minutes or until a toothpick inserted near the center comes out clean.

Cool for 10 minutes; remove from pan to a wire rack.

Costa Rican Coffee Panna Cotta with Bittersweet

Ingredients

- 2 teaspoons unflavored gelatin 1/4 cup dark rum
- 1 1/4 cups whipping cream
- 1/2 cup dark brown sugar
- 1 tablespoon instant espresso powder
- 1 cup coconut milk
- 1 teaspoon vanilla extract
- 1 cup sour cream
- 3/4 cup whipping cream
- 2 tablespoons dark colored corn syrup
- 8 ounces bittersweet chocolate, chopped
- 1 tablespoon dark rum
- 8 sprigs fresh mint for garnish

Directions

Sprinkle the unflavored gelatin over 1/4 cup of dark rum and allow to soften for 5 minutes. Meanwhile, stir together 1 1/4 cups of whipping cream, brown sugar, and espresso powder in a saucepan over medium-high heat.

Bring to a simmer, stirring until brown sugar has dissolved. Remove from heat, then whisk in gelatin mixture until dissolved. Whisk in the coconut milk, vanilla extract, and sour cream until smooth. Evenly divide the mixture between eight 3/4 cup custard cups or molds, cover each with plastic wrap, and chill at least 4 hours to overnight.

Bring 3/4 cup whipping cream and corn syrup to a simmer over medium-high heat. Once simmering, remove from heat, and stir in the chocolate until melted and smooth, about 2 minutes. Stir in 1 tablespoon of rum and set aside.

To serve, run a knife around the edge of each mold, then set each cup into a shallow bowl of hot water for 10 seconds to loosen.

Invert the mold over a serving plate and remove the panna cotta.

Spoon chocolate sauce around each panna cotta and garnish with a sprig of mint.

Toffee-Flavored Coffee

Ingredients

- 1/2 cup heavy whipping cream
- 1 tablespoon confectioners' sugar
- 1/2 cup milk chocolate toffee bits
- 5 cups hot brewed coffee
- 2 tablespoons butterscotch ice cream topping

Directions

In a small mixing bowl, beat cream until it begins to thicken. Add confectioners' sugar; beat until stiff peaks form. Stir toffee bits into coffee; let stand for 30 seconds.

Strain and discard any undissolved toffee bits. Pour coffee into mugs; top with whipped cream and drizzle with butterscotch topping.

Gingerbread Coffee

Ingredients

- 1/2 cup molasses
- 1/4 cup brown sugar
- 1/2 teaspoon baking soda
- 1 teaspoon ground ginger
- 3/4 teaspoon ground cinnamon
- 6 cups hot brewed coffee
- 1 cup half-and-half cream
- 1 teaspoon ground cloves
- 1 1/2 cups sweetened whipped cream

Directions

In a small bowl, mix together the molasses, brown sugar, baking soda, ginger and cinnamon until well blended. Cover and refrigerate for at least 10 minutes.

Add about a 1/4 cup of coffee to each cup, then stir in about a tablespoon of the spice mixture until dissolved.

Fill cup to within an inch of the top with coffee. Stir in half and half to taste, then garnish with whipped cream and a light dusting of cloves.

Easy Platz (Coffee Cake)

Ingredients

- 2 cups all-purpose flour
- 1 1/2 cups white sugar
- 2 teaspoons baking powder
- 1 teaspoon salt
- 2/3 cup margarine
- 2 eggs, beaten 2/3 cup milk
- 1 cup blackberries

Directions

Preheat oven to 350 degrees F (175 degrees C). Grease and flour a 9 inch square pan. In a large bowl, combine flour, sugar, baking powder and salt.

Cut in margarine until mixture resembles coarse crumbs. Set aside 3/4 cup of crumb mixture, to be used as a topping for the cake.
Mix eggs and milk together and then blend into remaining mixture in bowl. Spread batter into prepared pan. Sprinkle blackberries evenly over the top. Sprinkle reserved crumb mixture over fruit.

Pour batter into prepared pan. Bake in the preheated oven for 25 to 30 minutes, or until a toothpick inserted into the center of the cake comes out clean.

Quick Coffee Cake

Ingredients

- 1 1/2 cups all-purpose flour
- 1 1/2 teaspoons baking powder
- 6 tablespoons white sugar 1/2 teaspoon salt
- 1/3 cup shortening 1/2 cup milk
- 1 egg
- 1/2 teaspoon vanilla extract
- 2 tablespoons butter, melted 1/2 cup brown sugar
- 2 tablespoons all-purpose flour
- 1/2 teaspoon ground cinnamon

Directions

Preheat oven to 425 degrees F (220 degrees C). Grease and flour a 9 inch square pan. In a large bowl mix together the flour, baking powder, sugar and salt. Cut in the shortening with a pastry blender to the size of small peas.

In a separate small bowl, beat the egg well, then stir in the milk and vanilla. Add the egg-milk mixture to the flour mixture all at once. Stir carefully until just blended. Pour batter into prepared pan and spread evenly. Drizzle top with melted butter. In a small bowl mix together brown sugar, 2 tablespoons flour and 1/2 teaspoon cinnamon. Sprinkle on top of cake. Pour batter into prepared pan.

Bake in the preheated oven for 15 to 20 minutes, or until a toothpick inserted into the center of the cake comes outclean.

Blueberry Coffee Cake

Ingredients

- 1/4 cup butter, softened 2/3 cup sugar
- 1 egg
- 1 1/8 cups all-purpose flour, divided
- 1/2 teaspoon baking powder 1/4 teaspoon salt
- 1/2 cup milk
- 1 cup fresh or frozen blueberries
- 1 (3 ounce) package cream cheese, cubed
  TOPPING:
- 2 tablespoons all-purpose flour
- 2 tablespoons sugar
- 1 tablespoon cold butter

Directions

For batter, in a large mixing bowl, cream butter and sugar. Beat in egg. Combine 1 cup flour, baking powder and salt; gradually add to creamed mixture alternately with milk. Toss blueberries with remaining flour. Stir blueberries and cream cheese into creamed mixture (batter will be thick).

Transfer to a greased 8-in. square baking dish. For topping, in a small bowl, combine flour and sugar. Cut in butter until crumbly. Sprinkle over batter. Bake at 375 degrees F for 40-45 minutes or until a toothpick inserted near the center comes out clean. Cool on a wire rack.

Texas Praline Coffee Cake

Ingredients

- 2 cups baking mix (such as Bisquick ®)
- 1/2 cup brown sugar
- 3/4 cup chopped pecans
- 2 tablespoons instant coffee granules
- 1 large egg
- 1 cup butter flavored shortening, melted
- 1 teaspoon vanilla extract
- 1 cup buttermilk
- 1/4 cup brown sugar
- 1/4 cup chopped pecans
- 1/4 cup graham cracker crumbs 1/4 cup softened butter

Directions

Preheat an oven to 375 degrees F (190 degrees C). Grease and flour a 10 inch square cake pan. Mix baking mix, 1/2 cup brown sugar, 3/4 cup chopped pecans, and the instant coffee granules in a large bowl. Whisk together the egg, shortening, buttermilk, and vanilla in a separate large bowl. Stir the dry ingredients into the wet ingredients, mixing just untiln completely moistened.

Pour batter into prepared pan. Mix remaining 1/4 cup brown sugar, 1/4 cup chopped pecans, and the graham cracker crumbs in a small bowl. Sprinkle topping evenly over batter.

Bake in preheated oven until a toothpick inserted in the center comes out clean, about 20 to 25 minutes. Immediately dot top of cake with softened butter.

Peach Coffee Cake II

Ingredients

- 1 cup white sugar
- 1/2 cup butter, softened
- 1 cup sour cream
- 1 teaspoon vanilla extract
- 2 eggs, lightly beaten
- 2 cups all-purpose flour
- 1 1/2 teaspoons baking powder 1/2 teaspoon baking soda
- 1/2 teaspoon salt
- 4 cups peeled, pitted and sliced peaches
- 1/4 cup all-purpose flour 1/4 cup white sugar
- 1/4 cup chopped pecans
- 1 teaspoon ground cinnamon
- 3 tablespoons cold butter

Directions

Preheat oven to 325 degrees F (165 degrees C). Grease and flour a 9x13 inch baking pan. In a large bowl, cream together 1 cup sugar and 1/2 cup butter. Beat in sour cream, vanilla, and eggs.

Mix in flour, baking powder, baking soda, and salt. Spread 1/2 the batter into the baking pan. Layer with peaches, and top with remaining batter. In a small bowl, mix 1/4 cup flour, 1/4 cup sugar, pecans, and cinnamon.

Cut in cold butter until the mixture resembles coarse crumbs. Sprinkle evenly over the batter. Bake 45 minutes in the preheated oven, or until a knife inserted in the center comes out clean.

Rhubarb Crumb Coffee Cake

Ingredients

- 1/2 cup butter, softened
- 1 1/2 cups sugar
- 2 eggs
- 1 teaspoon vanilla extract
- 2 cups all-purpose flour
- 2 teaspoons ground cinnamon
- 1 teaspoon baking soda
- 1/4 teaspoon ground nutmeg
- 1 cup buttermilk
- 4 cups chopped fresh or frozen rhubarb
- TOPPING:
- 1 cup all-purpose flour
- 1/2 cup packed brown sugar
- 1 teaspoon ground cinnamon 1/2 cup cold butter

Directions

In a large mixing bowl, cream butter and sugar. Add eggs, one at a time, beating well after each addition. Beat in vanilla. Combine the dry ingredients; add to creamed mixture alternately with buttermilk. Stir in rhubarb. Pour into a greased 13-in. x 9-in. x 2-in. baking dish.

In a small bowl, combine the flour, brown sugar and cinnamon. Cut in butter until mixture resembles coarse crumbs. Sprinkle over batter. Bake at 350 degrees F for 45-55 minutes or until a toothpick inserted near the center comes out clean.

Cool on a wire rack.

Uncle Buc's Coffee Meat Rub

Ingredients

- 2 tablespoons ground coffee beans
- 2 tablespoons ground black pepper
- 1 1/2 tablespoons kosher salt
- 1/2 teaspoon cayenne pepper
- 1 tablespoon ground cumin

Directions

Preheat the oven broiler. Place the ground coffee on a sheet of aluminum foil, and place about 6 inches from the heat source. Broil for about 45 seconds, shaking the foil about every 10 seconds, or whenever you see smoke.

In a small bowl, stir together the coffee, black pepper, salt, cayenne pepper, and cumin. Rub into steaks, or pound in with a meat mallet. Grill as desired.

Blueberry Coffee Cake II

Ingredients

- 2 cups all-purpose flour
- 2 teaspoons baking powder 1/2 teaspoon salt
- 1/4 cup vegetable oil
- 3/4 cup white sugar
- 1 egg
- 1/2 cup milk
- 1 cup blueberries
- 1/3 cup all-purpose flour 1/2 cup white sugar
- 1/2 teaspoon ground cinnamon 1/4 cup butter, softened

Directions

Preheat oven to 375 degrees F (190 degrees C). Grease and flour a 9 inch pan. Sift together the flour, baking powder and salt. Set aside. In a large bowl, whisk together the oil, sugar and egg. Stir in the flour mixture alternately with the milk, mixing just until incorporated.

Fold in the blueberries. Pour batter into prepared pan. Cover with streusel topping. For the topping: In a bowl, combine 1/3 cup flour, cinnamon and ½ cup sugar. Cut in the butter until mixture resembles coarse crumbs.

Bake in the preheated oven for 45 minutes, or until a toothpick inserted into the center of the cake comes out clean. Allow to cool.

Streusel Coffee Cake

Ingredients

- 1 cup butter
- 2 cups white sugar
- 4 eggs
- 2 cups sour cream
- 2 teaspoons vanilla extract
- 4 cups all-purpose flour
- 2 teaspoons baking powder
- 2 teaspoons baking soda 1/2 cup white sugar
- 2 teaspoons ground cinnamon
- 1 cup chopped walnuts

Directions

Preheat oven to 350 degrees F (175 degrees C). Grease and flour a10 inch Bundt pan. In a medium bowl, mix the flour, baking powder and baking soda together and set aside. In a separate small bowl, combine 1/2 cup sugar, cinnamon, and nuts. Set aside. In a large bowl, cream butter and 2 cups white sugar until light and fluffy.

Add eggs, sour cream, and vanilla extract. Add flour mixture and beat until well combined. Pour half of batter into Bundt pan. Sprinkle half of the nut mixture on top of batter in pan. Add remaining batter, and sprinkle with the last of the nut mixture.

Bake at 350 degrees F (175 degrees C) for 45 to 60 minutes, or until a toothpick inserted into cake comes out clean.

Apple Coffee Cake

Ingredients

- 3 cups all-purpose flour
- 1 tablespoon baking powder
- 2 cups white sugar
- 1 cup vegetable oil
- 4 eggs
- 1/2 cup orange juice
- 4 apples - peeled, cored and sliced
- 5 tablespoons white sugar
- 5 tablespoons brown sugar
- 2 teaspoons ground cinnamon

Directions

Preheat oven to 350 degrees F (175 degrees C). Lightly grease a 10 inch tube pan. In a large bowl, stir together flour and baking powder. In a separate bowl, beat together 2 cups sugar, vegetable oil, eggs. Stir egg mixture into flour mixture, alternately with orange juice, until smooth.

In a small bowl, combine 5 tablespoons white sugar, 5 tablespoons brown sugar and 2 teaspoons cinnamon. Pour 1/2 of batter into prepared pan. Add 1/2 of the apples then 1/2 of the cinnamon sugar mixture.

Repeat laying with remaining ingredients. Bake in preheated oven until a toothpick inserted into center of cake comes out clean, about 50 to 70 minutes.
Let cool for 15 to 20 minutes, invert on a plate and serve.

Maple Nut Coffee Bread

Ingredients

- 1 tablespoon active dry yeast 1/4 cup warm water (105 degrees to 115 degrees)
- 1 cup warm milk (110 to 115 degrees F)
- 1/4 cup shortening 1/4 cup sugar
- 1 egg
- 1 teaspoon salt
- 1 teaspoon maple flavoring
- 1/8 teaspoon ground cardamom
- 3 1/2 cups all-purpose flour FILLING:
- 1 cup packed brown sugar
- 1/3 cup chopped pecans
- 1 teaspoon ground cinnamon
- 1 teaspoon maple flavoring
- 6 tablespoons butter or margarine, softened

  GLAZE:
- 1 1/2 cups confectioners' sugar
- 1/4 teaspoon maple flavored extract
- 2 tablespoons milk

Directions

In a mixing bowl, dissolve yeast in warm water. Add milk, shortening, sugar, egg, salt, maple flavoring and cardamom; mix well. Add the flour; beat until smooth. Turn onto a floured surface; knead until smooth and elastic, about 6-8 minutes. Place in a greased bowl, turning once to grease top.

Cover and let rise in a warm place until doubled, about 1 hour. Grease a baking sheet or 14-in. pizza pan or line with foil. For filling, combine the brown sugar, pecans, cinnamon and maple flavoring; set aside.

Punch dough down. Turn onto a lightly floured surface; divide into thirds. Roll each into a 14-in. circle; place one on prepared pan. Spread with a third of the butter; sprinkle with a third of the filling.

Top with a second circle of dough; top with butter and filling. Repeat.
Pinch to seal. Carefully place a glass in center of circle. With scissors, cut from outside edge just to the glass,forming 16 wedges.

Remove glass; twist each wedge five to six times. Pinchends to seal and tuck under. Cover and let rise until doubled, about 30 minutes.

Bake at 375 degrees F for 25-30minutes or until golden brown. For glaze, combine the sugar, maple flavoring and enough milk to achieve desired consistency; set aside. Carefully remove breadfrom pan by running a metal spatula under it to loosen.

Transfer to a wire rack. Drizzle with glaze. Cool completely or servewhile slightly warm.

Coffee Praline Muffins

Ingredients

- 1 3/4 cups all-purpose flour 1/3 cup brown sugar
- 1 tablespoon baking powder 1/4 teaspoon salt
- 1/2 cup chopped pecans 1/2 cup butter, melted 3/4 cup milk
- 2 tablespoons instant coffee powder
- 1 teaspoon vanilla extract 1 egg
- 1/8 cup brown sugar
- 2 tablespoons chopped pecans

Directions

Preheat oven to 375 degrees F (190 degrees C). Lightly grease 10 muffin cups. In a large mixing bowl, combine flour, 1/3 cup brown sugar, baking powder, salt and 1/2 cup chopped pecans. Add melted butter, milk, instant coffee, vanilla and egg. Mix until all of the dry ingredients are absorbed.

Fill the prepared muffin cups 2/3 full. Combine theremaining brown sugar and pecans, sprinkle over the tops of the muffins.

Bake at 375 degrees F (190 degrees C) for 18 to 20 minutes, or until a toothpick inserted into the center of a muffin comes out clean.

Cream Cheese Coffee Cake I

Ingredients

- 1/3 cup packed dark brown sugar
- 2 teaspoons unsweetened cocoa powder
- 1/3 cup chopped semisweet chocolate
- 1 teaspoon ground cinnamon 1/3 cup raisins
- 1/3 cup golden raisins
- 1/2 cup toasted walnuts, chopped
- 3/4 cup unsalted butter
- 1/2 (8 ounce) package cream cheese
- 1 cup packed brown sugar 1/3 cup white sugar
- 5 eggs
- 1 1/2 teaspoons vanilla extract
- 1 cup plain yogurt
- 3 1/4 cups all-purpose flour 1/4 teaspoon salt
- 1 tablespoon baking powder 1/2 teaspoon baking soda

Directions

Preheat oven to 350 degrees F (175 degrees C). Generously grease a 12 cup Bundt cake pan or a 9 or 10 inch tube pan. Soak raisins in warm water until plump. Drain and dry. Chop coarsely.

Mix with 1/3 cup dark brown sugar, cocoa, chocolate, cinnamon, and chopped nuts. You can also mince filling ingredients in a food processor for another texture.

Cream the unsalted butter with 1 cup brown sugar and white sugar until fluffy. Add cream cheese, and cream until blended. Add eggs and vanilla, and mix thoroughly.

Blend in yogurt or sour cream. Fold in flour, salt, baking powder, soda. Mix well on low speed of mixer. Spread one third batter in prepared pan. Top with some of the filling mixture. Layer in this fashion until filling and batter are used up.

Bake until done, 50 to 60 minutes. Cool in pan 10 minutes before removing.

Chocolate Chip Coffee Cake

Ingredients

- 1/2 cup butter, softened
- 1 cup white sugar
- 2 eggs
- 1 cup sour cream
- 1 teaspoon vanilla extract
- 2 1/2 cups all-purpose flour
- 1 1/2 teaspoons baking powder
- 1 teaspoon baking soda
- 1 cup semisweet chocolate chips 1/2 cup white sugar
- 1 teaspoon ground cinnamon

Directions

Preheat oven to 350 degrees F (175 degrees C) grease and flour a 9x13 inch pan. In a medium bowl, stir together the flour, baking powder and soda. Set aside.In a large bowl, cream the butter and 1 cup of sugar.

Add eggs, sour cream and vanilla. Mix well.Add the flour mixture and combine. Batter will be thick. In a separate bowl, combine chocolate chips, 1/2 cup sugar and cinnamon. Set aside.
Spread half of the cake batter in prepared 9x13 inch pan. Sprinkle half of the chocolate chip mixture over the batter.

Repeat with the remaining batter, and then the remaining chocolate chip mixture.Bake at 350 degrees F (175 degrees C) for 25-30 minutes or until a toothpick inserted near the center comes out clean.

Blueberry Coffee Cake III

Ingredients

- 1/4 cup butter
- 3/4 cup white sugar 1 egg
- 1/2 cup milk
- 2 cups all-purpose flour
- 2 teaspoons baking powder 1/2 teaspoon salt
- 2 cups blueberries
- 1/2 cup brown sugar
- 3 tablespoons all-purpose flour
- 1 teaspoon ground cinnamon 1/2 cup chopped pecans
- 3 tablespoons butter

Directions

Preheat oven to 375 degrees F (190 degrees C). Grease and flour a 9 inch springform pan. Sift together the flour, baking powder and salt. Set aside. In a large bowl, cream together the butter and sugar until light and fluffy. Beat in the egg. Beat in the flour mixture alternately with the milk, mixing just until incorporated. Stir in the blueberries.

Pour batter into prepared pan. In a small bowl, combine brown sugar, 3 tablespoons flour, cinnamon and chopped pecans. Cut in butter until crumbly. Sprinkle over the batter.
Bake in the preheated oven for 40 to 45 minutes, or until a toothpick inserted into the center of the cake comes out clean. Allow to cool.

Nutty Coffee Cake

Ingredients

- 2 1/2 cups buttermilk baking mix 1/3 cup white sugar
- 1 egg
- 3 tablespoons vegetable oil 2/3 cup milk
- 1/3 cup chopped walnuts, toasted 1/4 cup white sugar
- 1 tablespoon grated lemon zest

Directions

Preheat oven to 400 degrees F (200 degrees C). Grease and flour a 9 inch round pan. In a medium bowl, stir together the biscuit mix and 1/3 cup of sugar.

Add the egg, oil, and milk, mix until smooth. Spread evenly into the prepared pan. In another bowl, stir together the chopped nuts, 1/4 cup of sugar and lemon zest. Sprinkle this mixture over the batter in the pan. Bake in the preheated oven for 20 to 25 minutes, or until a toothpick inserted into the cake comes out clean.

Serve warm.

Eggless Coffee Cake

Ingredients

- 1 1/2 cups sifted unbleached all-purpose flour
- 2 teaspoons baking powder 1/2 teaspoon baking soda ¼ teaspoon salt
- 3/4 cup white sugar
- 3 teaspoons egg replacer (dry)
- 4 tablespoons water
- 1 cup sour cream substitute
- 1/2 teaspoon vanilla extract
- 1/4 cup fresh blueberries
- 1/4 cup chopped walnuts (optional)
- 5 tablespoons white sugar
- 2 tablespoons soy margarine
- 1/2 teaspoon ground cinnamon

Directions

Preheat oven to 350 degrees F (175 degrees C). Grease a 9x9 inch baking pan. In a large mixing bowl resift flour with the baking powder, baking soda, salt and 3/4 cup of sugar.

In a separate bowl combine the egg replacer and water (2 eggs' worth) and mix in sour creamsubstitute and vanilla. Pour the 'egg' mixture into the flour mixture and beat until smooth. Spread batter in baking pan.

Sprinkleblueberries (optional) and/or walnuts (optional) over the batter, and stir slightly so that they stay in the top layer.

In a small bowl, combine the 5 tablespoons sugar, margarine and cinnamon. Mix with a fork until mixture resembles cornmeal (not smooth). Sprinkle topping over batter. Bake in preheated oven for 20 to 25 minutes, or until a toothpick inserted into the center of the cake comes out clean.

Cool slightly before serving.

Coffee Souffle

Ingredients

- 1 1/2 cups brewed coffee 1/2 cup milk
- 1/2 cup white sugar, divided 1/4 teaspoon salt, divided
- 1 envelope (1 tablespoon) unflavored gelatin
- 3 eggs, separated
- 1/2 teaspoon vanilla extract

Directions

In the top of a double boiler over simmering water, combine coffee, milk, half the sugar, half the salt and gelatin.

Stir until solids are dissolved. Stir in remaining sugar and salt and the egg yolks. Cook and stir until thick and creamy, and mixture coats the back of a metal spoon.

Remove from heat. Whip the egg whites (with a pinch of salt, if desired) until stiff peaks form. Fold egg whites and vanilla into slightly cooled custard.

Pour into a serving dish or mold and chill until set.

Iced Coffee Slush

Ingredients

- 3 cups hot, strong brewed coffee
- 1 1/2 cups sugar
- 4 cups milk
- 2 cups half-and-half cream
- 1 1/2 teaspoons vanilla extract

Directions

In a freezer-safe bowl, stir coffee and sugar; until sugar is dissolved. Refrigerate until thoroughly chilled. Add the milk, cream and vanilla; freeze.

Remove from the freezer several hours before serving. Chop mixture until slushy; serve immediately.

Grandma Coffee's Beef Barley Vegetable Soup

Ingredients

- 1 pound beef stew meat, cut into bite-size pieces
- 6 cups water, plus more if desired
- 1 bay leaf
- 2 (14.5 ounce) cans canned diced tomatoes with their juice
- 4 carrots, cut into 1/4 inch rounds
- 4 stalks celery, cut into bite-size pieces
- 1 rutabaga, peeled and cut into bite-size pieces
- 1 large sweet onion, chopped
- 1/2 cup uncooked pearl barley
- 1 (10 ounce) package frozen white corn
- 1 (10 ounce) package frozen cut green beans
- 1 (10 ounce) package frozen baby lima beans (optional)
- seasoned salt (such as Morton® Nature's Seasons® Seasoning Blend) to taste

Directions

Place the beef, water, and bay leaf in a large soup pot over medium heat, and cook until the beef is very tender, about 1 hour. Stir in the tomatoes, carrots, celery, rutabaga, onion, and pearl barley, and simmer until the vegetables are tender, about 30 minutes.

Add the frozen white corn, green beans, and lima beans, season to taste, and simmer an additional 15 to 20 minutes, until the frozen vegetables are tender.
Add more water if the soup is too thick.

Coffee Cream Cheese Spread

Ingredients

- 2 (3 ounce) packages cream cheese, softened
- 1/4 cup confectioners' sugar 1/2 teaspoon instant coffee granules

Directions

In a small mixing bowl, beat cream cheese, confectioners' sugar and coffee granules until light and fluffy.

Serve with bread, bagels or toast. Store in the refrigerator.

Jamaica Coffee

Ingredients

- 3/4 fluid ounce dark rum
- 3/4 fluid ounce coffee flavored liqueur
- 1 cup brewed coffee
- 2 tablespoons whipped cream
- 1 chocolate covered coffee bean

Directions

Pour rum and coffee liqueur into a decorative coffee glass. Fill glass with hot coffee.
Top with a dollop of whipped cream and garnish with a coffee bean.

Potato Coffee Cake

Ingredients

- 3/4 cup dry potato flakes
- 1 cup boiling water
- 1 cup warm milk
- 3 tablespoons butter, softened
- 2 eggs
- 1 cup white sugar
- 4 1/2 cups bread flour
- 1 (.25 ounce) package active dry yeast
- 3 tablespoons white sugar
- 1/2 teaspoon ground cinnamon
- 3 tablespoons butter, melted

Directions

In a small bowl, dissolve potato flakes in boiling water. Let stand until lukewarm, about 15 minutes.

Place ingredients in the pan of the bread machine in the order recommended by the manufacturer.
Select Dough/Manual cycle; press Start. The mixing and first rise of the dough will be completed in the bread machine.

When Dough/Manual cycle is finished, remove dough and briefly knead on a floured board. Divide dough into 3 round loaves and place in three lightly greased 8 inch pie pans.

Cover and let raiseuntil doubled in size, about 60 minutes. Meanwhile, preheat oven to 350 degrees F (175 degrees C).

In a small bowl, combine 3 tablespoons sugar with 1/2 teaspoon cinnamon. Brush risen loaves with melted butter and sprinkle with cinnamon sugar mixture.

Bake in preheated oven for 20 minutes, or until golden brown.

Overnight Berry Coffee Cake

Ingredients

- 2 cups all-purpose flour
- 1 cup sugar
- 1/2 cup packed brown sugar
- 1 teaspoon baking powder
- 1 teaspoon baking soda
- 1 teaspoon ground cinnamon 1/2 teaspoon salt
- 1 cup buttermilk
- 2/3 cup butter or margarine, melted
- 2 eggs, beaten
- 1 cup fresh or frozen raspberries or blueberries
- TOPPING:
- 1/2 cup packed brown sugar 1/2 cup chopped nuts
- 1 teaspoon ground cinnamon

Directions

In a large bowl, combine flours, sugars, baking powder, baking soda, cinnamon and salt. In a separate bowl, combine buttermilk, butter and eggs; add to dry ingredients and mix until well blended. Fold in berries. Pour into a greased 13-in. x 9-in. x 2-in. baking pan.

Combine topping ingredients; sprinkle over batter. Cover and efrigerate several hours or overnight.

Uncover and bake at 350 degrees F for 45-50 minutes or until cake tests done.

Strawberry Coffee Cake

Ingredients

- 1 cup all-purpose flour 1/2 cup sugar
- 2 teaspoons baking powder 1/2 teaspoon salt
- 1 egg
- 1/2 cup milk
- 2 tablespoons butter, melted
- 1 1/2 cups sliced fresh strawberries

  TOPPING:
- 1/2 cup all-purpose flour 1/2 cup sugar
- 1/4 cup cold butter
- 1/4 cup chopped pecans

Directions

In a large bowl, combine the flour, sugar, baking powder and salt. In another bowl, beat the egg, milk and butter. Stir into dry ingredients just until moistened. Pour into a greased 8-in. square baking dish. Top with strawberries.

For topping, combine flour and sugar in a bowl; cut in butter until crumbly. Stir in pecans if desired; sprinkle over strawberries.

Bake at 375 degrees F for 30-35 minutes or until a toothpick inserted near the center comes out clean. Cut into squares; serve warm.

Coffee McAvee

Ingredients

- 11 (1.5 fluid ounce) jiggers coffee flavored liqueur
- 1/4 cup white sugar
- 10 (1.5 fluid ounce) jiggers 151 proof rum
- 5 cups vanilla ice cream
- 5 cups hot, brewed coffee

Directions

Pour 2 jiggers of coffee flavored liqueur into a saucer. Spread sugar out on a separate saucer. Dip each glass into the liqueur and then into the sugar to coat the rim.

Pour 1 jigger of rum into each glass. Light the rum on fire using a long match and allow it to burn the sugar around the rim of the glass until it has turned to caramel, about 1 minute.Extinguish the fire in each glass with a 1/2 cup sized scoop of ice cream.

Pour 1 jigger of coffee liqueur over the ice cream, and top off the glass with hot coffee.

Coffee Ice Cream Fudge Cake

Ingredients

- 1/2 cup light corn syrup
- 1 cup heavy cream
- 10 ounces semisweet chocolate, chopped
- 16 graham crackers, broken into 1/2-inch pieces
- 1 cup toasted almonds
- 3 tablespoons white sugar 1/2 cup melted butter
- 1 1/2 quarts coffee ice cream, softened
- 1 (7 ounce) jar marshmallow creme
- 2 cups miniature marshmallows

Directions

To make fudge sauce, combine heavy cream and corn syrup in heavy saucepan. Bring to a boil, remove from heat, add chocolate and whisk until smooth. Refrigerate until cool, about 45 minutes.

To make ice cream cake, preheat oven to 350 degrees F (175 degrees C). Finely grind graham crackers and almonds in foodprocessor or blender. Stir in sugar. Add butter and process until moist crumbs form. Press mixture into bottom and sides of 9 inch spring form pan. Bake until golden, about 12 minutes.

Allow to cool, then spread 2 cups softened ice cream over crust. Spoon 3/4 cup fudge sauce over ice cream. Freeze until set, then repeat layering. Cover and freeze 8 hours or overnight. Refrigerate remaining fudge sauce.

The next day, preheat the oven broiler. Warm the remaining fudge sauce in the microwave or a small saucepan. Place the cake pan on a cookie sheet. Spread the marshmallow creme over cake and sprinkle miniature marshmallows on top.

Place under broiler until marshmallows are deep brown. Loosen cake with knife and remove sides of pan.
Serve immediately with warmed fudge sauce.

Deep-Dish Cheesecake Coffee Cake

Ingredients

- 3 cups buttermilk baking mix 1/4 cup white sugar
- 1/4 cup butter, melted 1/2 cup milk
- 1/2 cup white sugar
- 1/2 teaspoon vanilla extract
- 2 eggs
- 1 (8 ounce) package cream cheese, softened
- 1/4 cup strawberry, apricot or raspberry preserves

Directions

Preheat oven to 375 degrees F (190 degrees C). To make the crust, in a medium bowl, combine the baking mix, ¼ cup sugar, melted butter and milk. Stir until a dough forms, then turn the dough out onto a clean surface that has been dusted with some baking mix. Knead for 30 turns.

Pat the dough into the bottom and up the sides of an ungreased 9 inch round cake pan. In the same bowl, beat together the remaining 1/2 cup sugar, vanilla, eggs and cream cheese. Pour over the dough in the pan.

Bake for 30 minutes in the preheated oven, until the edges are golden and the filling is set. Allow the coffee cake to cool for 10 minutes, then spread the fruit preserves over the top.